THE JPS B'NAI MITZVAH TORAH COMMENTARY

Tsav (Leviticus 6:1–8:36)
Haftarah (Jeremiah 7:21–8:3; 9:22–23)

Rabbi Jeffrey K. Salkin

The Jewish Publication Society · Philadelphia
University of Nebraska Press · Lincoln

INTRODUCTION

News flash: the most important thing about becoming bar or bat mitzvah isn't the party. Nor is it the presents. Nor even being able to celebrate with your family and friends—as wonderful as those things are. Nor is it even standing before the congregation and reading the prayers of the liturgy—as important as that is.

No, the most important thing about becoming bar or bat mitzvah is sharing Torah with the congregation. And why is that? Because of all Jewish skills, that is the most important one.

Here is what is true about rites of passage: you can tell what a culture values by the tasks it asks its young people to perform on their way to maturity. In American culture, you become responsible for driving, responsible for voting, and yes, responsible for drinking responsibly.

In some cultures, the rite of passage toward maturity includes some kind of trial, or a test of strength. Sometimes, it is a kind of "outward bound" camping adventure. Among the Maasai tribe in Africa, it is traditional for a young person to hunt and kill a lion. In some Hispanic cultures, fifteen year-old girls celebrate the *quinceañera*, which marks their entrance into maturity.

What is Judaism's way of marking maturity? It combines both of these rites of passage: *responsibility* and *test*. You show that you are on your way to becoming a *responsible* Jewish adult through a public *test* of strength and knowledge—reading or chanting Torah, and then teaching it to the congregation.

This is the most important Jewish ritual mitzvah (commandment), and that is how you demonstrate that you are, truly, bar or bat mitzvah—old enough to be responsible for the mitzvot.

What Is Torah?

So, what exactly is the Torah? You probably know this already, but let's review.

The Torah (teaching) consists of "the five books of Moses," sometimes also called the *chumash* (from the Hebrew word *chameish,* which means "five"), or, sometimes, the Greek word Pentateuch (which means "the five teachings").

Here are the five books of the Torah, with their common names and their Hebrew names.

> **Genesis (The beginning), which in Hebrew is Bere'shit (from the first words—"When God began to create").** Bere'shit spans the years from Creation to Joseph's death in Egypt. Many of the Bible's best stories are in Genesis: the creation story itself; Adam and Eve in the Garden of Eden; Cain and Abel; Noah and the Flood; and the tales of the Patriarchs and Matriarchs, Abraham, Isaac, Jacob, Sarah, Rebekah, Rachel, and Leah. It also includes one of the greatest pieces of world literature, the story of Joseph, which is actually the oldest complete novel in history, comprising more than one-quarter of all Genesis.

> **Exodus (Getting out), which in Hebrew is Shemot (These are the names).** Exodus begins with the story of the Israelite slavery in Egypt. It then moves to the rise of Moses as a leader, and the Israelites' liberation from slavery. After the Israelites leave Egypt, they experience the miracle of the parting of the Sea of Reeds (or "Red Sea"); the giving of the Ten Commandments at Mount Sinai; the idolatry of the Golden Calf; and the design and construction of the Tabernacle and of the ark for the original tablets of the law, which our ancestors carried with them in the desert. Exodus also includes various ethical and civil laws, such as "You shall not wrong a stranger or oppress him, for you were strangers in the land of Egypt" (22:20).

> **Leviticus (about the Levites), or, in Hebrew, Va-yikra' (And God called).** It goes into great detail about the kinds of sacrifices that the ancient Israelites brought as offerings; the laws of ritual purity; the animals that were permitted and forbidden for eating (the beginnings of the tradition of kashrut, the Jewish dietary laws); the diagnosis of various skin diseases; the ethical laws of holiness; the ritual calendar of the Jewish year; and various agricultural laws concerning the treatment of the Land of Israel. Leviticus is basically the manual of ancient Judaism.

- Numbers (because the book begins with the census of the Israelites), or, in Hebrew, Be-midbar (In the wilderness). The book describes the forty years of wandering in the wilderness and the various rebellions against Moses. The constant theme: "Egypt wasn't so bad. Maybe we should go back." The greatest rebellion against Moses was the negative reports of the spies about the Land of Israel, which discouraged the Israelites from wanting to move forward into the land. For that reason, the "wilderness generation" must die off before a new generation can come into maturity and finish the journey.
- Deuteronomy (The repetition of the laws of the Torah), or, in Hebrew, Devarim (The words). The final book of the Torah is, essentially, Moses's farewell address to the Israelites as they prepare to enter the Land of Israel. Here we find various laws that had been previously taught, though sometimes with different wording. Much of Deuteronomy contains laws that will be important to the Israelites as they enter the Land of Israel—laws concerning the establishment of a monarchy and the ethics of warfare. Perhaps the most famous passage from Deuteronomy contains the *Shema,* the declaration of God's unity and uniqueness, and the *Ve-ahavta,* which follows it. Deuteronomy ends with the death of Moses on Mount Nebo as he looks across the Jordan Valley into the land that he will not enter.

Jews read the Torah in sequence—starting with Bere'shit right after Simchat Torah in the autumn, and then finishing Devarim on the following Simchat Torah. Each Torah portion is called a parashah (division; sometimes called a *sidrah,* a place in the order of the Torah reading). The stories go around in a full circle, reminding us that we can always gain more insights and more wisdom from the Torah. This means that if you don't "get" the meaning this year, don't worry—it will come around again.

And What Else? The Haftarah

We read or chant the Torah from the Torah scroll—the most sacred thing that a Jewish community has in its possession. The Torah is written without vowels, and the ability to read it and chant it is part of the challenge and the test.

But there is more to the synagogue reading. Every Torah reading has an accompanying haftarah reading. Haftarah means "conclusion," because there was once a time when the service actually ended with that reading. Some scholars believe that the reading of the haftarah originated at a time when non-Jewish authorities outlawed the reading of the Torah, and the Jews read the haftarah sections instead. In fact, in some synagogues, young people who become bar or bat mitzvah read very little Torah and instead read the entire haftarah portion.

The haftarah portion comes from the Nevi'im, the prophetic books, which are the second part of the Jewish Bible. It is either read or chanted from a Hebrew Bible, or maybe from a booklet or a photocopy.

The ancient sages chose the haftarah passages because their themes reminded them of the words or stories in the Torah text. Sometimes, they chose *haftarah* with special themes in honor of a festival or an upcoming festival.

Not all books in the prophetic section of the Hebrew Bible consist of prophecy. Several are historical. For example:

The book of Joshua tells the story of the conquest and settlement of Israel.

The book of Judges speaks of the period of early tribal rulers who would rise to power, usually for the purpose of uniting the tribes in war against their enemies. Some of these leaders are famous: Deborah, the great prophetess and military leader, and Samson, the biblical strong man.

The books of Samuel start with Samuel, the last judge, and then move to the creation of the Israelite monarchy under Saul and David (approximately 1000 BCE).

The books of Kings tell of the death of King David, the rise of King Solomon, and how the Israelite kingdom split into the Northern Kingdom of Israel and the Southern Kingdom of Judah (approximately 900 BCE).

And then there are the books of the prophets, those spokesmen for God whose words fired the Jewish conscience. Their names are immortal: Isaiah, Jeremiah, Ezekiel, Amos, Hosea, among others.

Someone once said: "There is no evidence of a biblical prophet ever being invited back a second time for dinner." Why? Because the prophets were tough. They had no patience for injustice, apathy, or hypocrisy. No one escaped their criticisms. Here's what they taught:

> God commands the Jews to behave decently toward one another. In fact, God cares more about basic ethics and decency than about ritual behavior.
> God chose the Jews *not* for special privileges, but for special duties to humanity.
> As bad as the Jews sometimes were, there was always the possibility that they would improve their behavior.
> As bad as things might be now, it will not always be that way. Someday, there will be universal justice and peace. Human history is moving forward toward an ultimate conclusion that some call the Messianic Age: a time of universal peace and prosperity for the Jewish people and for all the people of the world.

Your Mission—To Teach Torah to the Congregation

On the day when you become bar or bat mitzvah, you will be reading, or chanting, Torah—in Hebrew. You will be reading, or chanting, the haftarah—in Hebrew. That is the major skill that publicly marks the becoming of bar or bat mitzvah. But, perhaps even more important than that, you need to be able to teach something about the Torah portion, and perhaps the haftarah as well.

And that is where this book comes in. It will be a very valuable resource for you, and your family, in the b'nai mitzvah process.

Here is what you will find in it:

> A brief **summary** of every Torah portion. This is a basic overview of the portion; and, while it might not refer to everything in the Torah portion, it will explain its most important aspects.
> A list of the **major ideas** in the Torah portion. The purpose: to make the Torah portion real, in ways that we can relate to. Every Torah portion contains unique ideas, and when you put all

of those ideas together, you actually come up with a list of Judaism's most important ideas.

> Two *divrei Torah* ("words of Torah," or "sermonettes") for each portion. These *divrei Torah* explain significant aspects of the Torah portion in accessible, reader-friendly language. Each *devar Torah* contains references to **traditional** Jewish sources (those that were written before the modern era), as well as **modern** sources and quotes. We have searched, far and wide, to find sources that are unusual, interesting, and not just the "same old stuff" that many people already know about the Torah portion. Why did we include these minisermons in the volume? Not because we want you to simply copy those sermons and pass them off as your own (that would be cheating), though you are free to quote from them. We included them so that you can see what is possible—how you can try to make meaning for yourself out of the words of Torah.

> **Connections:** This is perhaps the most valuable part. It's a list of questions that you can ask yourself, or that others might help you think about—any of which can lead to the creation of your *devar Torah.*

Note: you don't have to like everything that's in a particular Torah portion. Some aren't that loveable. Some are hard to understand; some are about religious practices that people today might find confusing, and even offensive; some contain ideas that we might find totally outmoded.

But this doesn't have to get in the way. After all, most kids spend a lot of time thinking about stories that contain ideas that modern people would find totally bizarre. Any good medieval fantasy story falls into that category.

And we also believe that, if you spend just a little bit of time with those texts, you can begin to understand what the author was trying to say.

This volume goes one step further. Sometimes, the haftarah comes off as a second thought, and no one really thinks about it. We have tried to solve that problem by including a **summary** of each haftarah, and then a mini-sermon on the haftarah. This will help you learn how these sacred words are relevant to today's world, and even to your own life.

All Bible quotations come from the NJPS translation, which is found in the many different editions of the JPS TANAKH; in the Conservative movement's *Etz Hayim: Torah and Commentary;* in the Reform movement's *Torah: A Modern Commentary;* and in other Bible commentaries and study guides.

How Do I Write a *Devar Torah?*

It really is easier than it looks.

There are many ways of thinking about the *devar Torah.* It is, of course, a short sermon on the meaning of the Torah (and, perhaps, the haftarah) portion. It might even be helpful to think of the *devar Torah* as a "book report" on the portion itself.

The most important thing you can know about this sacred task is: *Learn* the words. *Love* the words. Teach people what it could mean to *live* the words.

Here's a basic outline for a *devar Torah:*

"My Torah portion is (name of portion) _____,
   from the book of _____, chapter
   _____."

"In my Torah portion, we learn that_____
   (Summary of portion)
"For me, the most important lesson of this Torah portion is (what
   is the best thing in the portion? Take the portion as a whole;
   your *devar Torah* does not have to be only, or specifically, on the
   verses that you are reading).
"As I learned my Torah portion, I found myself wondering:
   ➤ *Raise a question that the Torah portion itself raises.*
   ➤ *"Pick a fight"* with the portion. Argue with it.
   ➤ *Answer a question* that is listed in the "Connections" section of
      each Torah portion.
   ➤ *Suggest a question to your rabbi* that you would want the rabbi
      to answer in his or her own *devar Torah* or sermon.

"I have lived the values of the Torah by _____
(here, you can talk about how the Torah portion relates to your
own life. If you have done a mitzvah project, you can talk about
that here).

How To Keep It from Being Boring
(and You from Being Bored)

Some people just don't like giving traditional speeches. From our per-
spective, that's really okay. Perhaps you can teach Torah in a different
way—one that makes sense to you.

> Write an "open letter" to one of the characters in your Torah por-
  tion. "Dear Abraham: I hope that your trip to Canaan was not too
  hard . . ." "Dear Moses: Were you afraid when you got the Ten
  Commandments on Mount Sinai? I sure would have been . . ."
> Write a news story about what happens. Imagine yourself to
  be a television or news reporter. "Residents of neighboring cities were horrified yesterday as the wicked cities of Sodom and
  Gomorrah were burned to the ground. Some say that God was
  responsible . . ."
> Write an imaginary interview with a character in your Torah portion.
> Tell the story from the point of view of another character, or a mi-
  nor character, in the story. For instance, tell the story of the Gar-
  den of Eden from the point of view of the serpent. Or the story
  of the Binding of Isaac from the point of view of the ram, which
  was substituted for Isaac as a sacrifice. Or perhaps the story of
  the sale of Joseph from the point of view of his coat, which was
  stripped off him and dipped in a goat's blood.
> Write a poem about your Torah portion.
> Write a song about your Torah portion.
> Write a play about your Torah portion, and have some friends act
  it out with you.
> Create a piece of artwork about your Torah portion.

The bottom line is: Make this a joyful experience. Yes—it could
even be fun.

The Very Last Thing You Need to Know at This Point

The Torah scroll is written without vowels. Why? Don't *sofrim* (Torah scribes) know the vowels?

Of course they do.

So, why do they leave the vowels out?

One reason is that the Torah came into existence at a time when sages were still arguing about the proper vowels, and the proper pronunciation.

But here is another reason: The Torah text, as we have it today, and as it sits in the scroll, is actually *an unfinished work*. Think of it: the words are just sitting there. Because they have no vowels, it is as if they have no voice.

When we read the Torah publicly, we give voice to the ancient words. And when we find meaning in those ancient words, and we talk about those meanings, those words jump to life. They enter our lives. They make our world deeper and better.

Mazal tov to you, and your family. This is your journey toward Jewish maturity. Love it.

THE TORAH

❖ Tsav: Leviticus 6:1–8:36

The "yuck" theme continues: the ancient Israelite sacrificial system. In this Torah portion we read about the burnt offering (*olah*), the grain offering (*minchah*), the offering that would purify the worshiper of sin (*chattat*), the offering of reparation (*asham*), and the offering of well-being (*zevach shelamim*).

The portion concludes with a description of the way that the priests (*kohanim*) are inducted into their sacred duties.

There are important themes that emerge from all this description of sacrifices and priests.

Summary

> ‣ The burnt offering (*olah*, sometimes translated as "holocaust")
> must be burned entirely. It must be kept burning on the altar all
> night long, and the fire of the altar must burn perpetually. More-
> over, the priest is responsible for carrying the ashes of the sacri-
> fice outside the camp to a pure place. (6:1–6)
> ‣ The grain offering (*minchah*) is presented to the Lord, but Aaron
> and his sons eat what is left over from the offering. (6:7–11)
> ‣ The reparation offering (*asham*) is intended as a way to purify the
> worshiper of the wrongs that he or she has committed. (7:1–10)
> ‣ The elaborate rituals of investiture (ordaining) of the priests
> are filled with sacrificial offerings. An important part of the rit-
> ual is to put the blood of a sacrifice on Aaron's right ear, his right
> thumb, and the big toe of his right foot. (8:1–36)

The Big Ideas

> **The fire that burns perpetually on the altar symbolizes Judaism—and the Jewish people.** In this way, the perpetual fire is like the burning bush that Moses saw, and the eternal light (*ner tamid*) in synagogues. These are all sources of warmth and light that will last forever—like Judaism and the Jews.

> **No one is too special to be involved in small things.** The priest is not exempt from the "dirty work" of Jewish living. He, and not a subordinate, is responsible for cleaning up from the sacrifice. This ensures that the priests will always remember to be holy.

> **We need to love the Jewish past.** The leftover ashes of the sacrifice are also holy. The Jewish past, even though it is history, is as important as the Jewish present and the Jewish future.

> **Judaism is about community.** The sacrifices are not only for God. In fact, they are mostly connected with our acts of eating. Eating is a way for people to feel a sense of community.

> **Judaism says that you can move on from doing something wrong.** Judaism does not believe in simply feeling guilty, it teaches that you can make restitution. In ancient days, that was in the form of a sacrificial offering. Nowadays, it can take the form of an apology and/or somehow making up for what you have done.

> **Judaism is connected to the body.** The ritual of investiture of the priests involves three parts of the body: the ear, the thumb, and the big toe. Each body part symbolizes an essential part of living: hearing, action, and walking.

Divrei Torah
DOING THE CHORES

Chores. Who needs them? And yet we all have them: doing the dishes, taking out the garbage, walking the dog, shoveling snow, cleaning our rooms. Doing chores is one of the most basic aspects of living as part of a family. No one can do it all, and everyone needs to pitch in.

It turns out that there were chores—even in the ancient Tabernacle. And just wait until you learn who had to do them.

There was a sacrificial offering called the *olah*, the burnt offering. The priest, dressed in his fancy linen garments, took the ashes and placed them next to the altar. He then took off his garments, changed into other clothing, and carried the ashes outside the camp (6:2–4).

Your synagogue probably has a custodian who cleans up after people. (Quick: what's his or her name?) We tend to think of janitors and custodians as, well, "lowly" people, and we sometimes look down on them. This, of course, is wrong. The Bible, too, mentions the "wood choppers and water drawers." But when it came to the Tabernacle the cleanup crew consisted not of the lowliest Israelites, but of the holiest—the priests themselves.

What do we learn from this? No matter how important the priest might have been, he still had to get "down and dirty." It was a lesson in humility. In fact, the priests actually competed to do this work! There was so much competition that two priests once ran up the ramp of the ancient Temple, fighting to get to the top, and one of them pushed the other and he broke his leg. Here's how the early sages said the problem was fixed: "There was a daily lottery to see who would have the privilege of climbing up the ramp to the top of the altar and carrying away the ashes."

We tend to distrust religious leaders who live in big mansions, have fancy cars and vacation homes, and dress a little too well. We want to see humility, not arrogance. After all, "to walk humbly" is the famous teaching of the prophets, and a prime characteristic of Moses.

During the Holocaust, the great German rabbi Leo Baeck was a prisoner in the Theresienstadt concentration camp. He was the undisputed leader of all German Jewry—a man so respected that even

Nazis officers showed deference to him. Rabbi Baeck stayed with his community in Berlin, even though he had a chance to leave, and then accompanied them to that awful place.

And yet, what did he do in the concentration camp? He became a "horse," pulling a garbage wagon, like other prisoners. Rabbi Baeck said: "I was quite happy doing this. The other 'horse' harnessed to the same cart was a distinguished philosopher. We had wonderful conversations about ethics and religion as we dragged the refuse through the mud."

Rabbi Baeck knew that there was dignity even in demeaning work. It is a lesson that we can all learn.

A JEWISH ANATOMY LESSON

Ask any rabbi or cantor about the ceremony in which he or she became a rabbi or cantor. They will probably tell you something like this: There was a huge ordination ceremony, perhaps in a large, prominent synagogue. A seminary official called each candidate up by name. The president or chancellor said some private words to the candidate, blessed him or her, and that's it. That person then became a rabbi or a cantor. Mazel tov!

Not bad, especially when you compare it to the way that the priests were ordained in biblical times. An animal was slaughtered, and a little bit of blood was placed on the middle part of Aaron's right ear, and the thumb of his right hand, and then the big toe of his right foot—and then he was a priest. His sons went through the same ordination rituals.

If you're left handed, you're probably feeling a little "left out" right now. Yes, the Bible seems to be discriminating against left-handed people. Equality and inclusion as we know it was not fully developed back then. But, getting past the bias, an important lesson is to be learned from this ancient ceremony: the three body parts—the ear, thumb, and toe—are essential to being a Jew, and being human.

Let's start with the ear. Remember that the central statement of Jewish faith begins this way: *Shema Yisrael* (Hear, Israel). You need to be able to listen to people and really hear what they are saying. This does not mean that you have to agree with everything that everyone says; sometimes it is simply enough to pay attention to others. And we not only have to train ourselves to really listen; we also have to train ourselves to hear—to hear the right things, not to listen to gossip, and to learn how to figure out the truth.

Next, there is the thumb. Having a thumb is one of those things that make us human and able to function as humans. The thumb stands for the ability to act.

Finally, there is the big toe. Funny thing about the big toe; we usually ignore it, unless someone steps on it or we stub it. Without our big toes, we would not be able to balance ourselves. But, more than this, pay attention to how you walk. What's the first part of the body that moves when you move forward? Right—the big toe. Movement and balance.

So, yes, in order to be a fully functional Jewish person you need those body parts. The ancient Jewish philosopher Philo teaches: "The fully consecrated must be pure in words and actions and in life; for words are judged by hearing, the hand is the symbol of action, and the foot symbolizes the pilgrimage of life."

But, beyond that, those body parts are necessary for being human. As contemporary Jewish educator Sorel Goldberg Loeb writes: "The priest is smeared with blood to remind him of his bond with all life. But the parts of his body that are marked are those that distinguish him from and elevate him above the animals."

Connections

> What do you do that is considered menial? Why is it important?

> How can we make sure that Judaism lasts forever?

> What ways can you show loyalty to the Jewish past, present, and future?

> What are some ways that you have felt a sense of community in eating with others?

> What are ways that you have made up for some wrongs you have done?

> In what ways do you use your ears, thumbs, and toes "Jewishly"?

THE HAFTARAH

❖ Tsav: Jeremiah 7:21–8:3; 9:22–23

Let's remember the word "jeremiad." A "jeremiad" is a hot, angry, rant that someone delivers in the hope of changing society. The word comes from the prophet Jeremiah. Jeremiah, who preached during the final days of the Southern Kingdom of Judah, was sure of many things. Among them was his belief that sacrifices alone could not make God happy. Rather, those sacrifices had to be accompanied by acts of justice.

It's the subject of sacrifice that links this haftarah back to the Torah portion, which is a continuation of Leviticus's description of the ancient sacrificial system. Jeremiah is warning the people: if you keep worshiping idols in the Temple, and if you keep sacrificing your children to idols in the valleys of Jerusalem, God will destroy Jerusalem, and you will all be destroyed as well.

It gets even worse. Jeremiah tells the people that even after they have been killed, their bodies will be pulled from their graves and left to rot under the sun and the stars—under the "hosts of heaven," which they have worshiped.

Now, you know why they call these kinds of proclamations "jeremiads." Jeremiah was angry. He must have believed in shock therapy. Although not all his message is so negative, much of it is—just like political advertising today!

Idols Are More Than Statues

The prophets were soldiers in a war—and that war was against idolatry. As the writer Norman Podhoretz said: "This was a war to establish the truth of the great revelation—namely, that there was only one God, not many gods, that you couldn't see him, you couldn't make a picture of him, you couldn't make a statue of him to which you would then bow down."

Yes, making a god with your own hands was surely idolatry. But it didn't end there. Jeremiah didn't like the way that the Judeans were worshiping God. He and the other prophets thought that the worship of *anything* other than God was idolatry.

Jeremiah says: "Thus said the Lord: Let not the wise man glory in his wisdom; let not the strong man glory in his strength; let not the rich man glory in his riches" (Jer. 9:23). It's a continuation of the theme in last week's haftarah portion, on the danger of self-worship.

Sometimes, people think their intellect is the most important thing there is, and that leads to abuses of knowledge. Sometimes, people think power is the most important thing, and that leads to abuses of power. It's not only nations that do this; individuals do it as well. (Think of the athletic coach who abuses his or her power over team members.) And, sometimes, people think that their money and what it can buy is the most important thing. (Think of how much some families spend on bar or bat mitzvah celebrations!)

Rabbi Dini Lewittes puts it this way: "Are we not guilty of making academic achievement, political power and material wealth the ultimate values of our Jewish community? Perhaps if we listen carefully to Jeremiah's moving words, we can create a community that reflects the most cherished values of our people: justice, kindness and equity."

So, what is the real way to worship God, asks Jeremiah? To reject idolatry. The Talmud teaches: "Whoever rejects idolatry has already observed the entire Torah." We worship God by knowing that "I the Lord act with kindness, justice, and equity in the world; for in these I delight—declares the Lord" (9:22–23).

Act that way; that is all that God really wants us to do.

❖ Notes

❖ Notes

CPSIA information can be obtained
at www.ICGtesting.com
Printed in the USA
LVHW091626011218
598911LV00001B/69/P